MW00881246

PHILLIP LINDSAY

by
Ryan Jacobson

Minneapolis, Minnesota

ABOUT THE AUTHOR

Ryan Jacobson is an award-winning author and presenter. He has written more than 50 titles—from comic books to "choose your path" adventures. He prides himself on writing high-interest books for children and adults alike, so he can talk picture books in kindergarten, ghost stories in high school, and other fun stuff in between. Ryan greatly enjoys sharing his knowledge of writing and book publishing at schools and special events. Ryan lives with his wife and two sons.

Acknowledgments
Special thanks to everyone who helped with the creation and promotion of this book, especially Natalie Fowler, Jessica Freeburg, and Cheri Jacobson.

Proofread by Emily Beaumont

Cover design by Ryan Jacobson and germancreative

Phillip Lindsay photograph (front cover) by Ric Tapia. Copyright 2019 The Associated Press. Football image (back cover) copyright David Lee / Shutterstock.com. For additional photography credits, see page 104.

The information presented here is accurate to the best of our knowledge. However, the information is not guaranteed. It is solely the reader's responsibility to verify the information before relying upon it.

This book is not affiliated with, authorized, endorsed, or sponsored by the National Football League, its players, or anyone involved with the league.

The use of any trademarks is for identification and reference purposes only and does not imply any association with the trademark holder.

TABLE OF CONTENTS

PROLOGUE

Phillip Lindsay was as surprised as anyone. He was standing on the field of Broncos Stadium at Mile High, in front of 76,000 cheering fans. Phillip imagined that he would see action during the game on kickoffs and punts. He didn't know that the team intended to use him on offense.

Yet there he was, 8 minutes into his first game, and Denver had moved the football into scoring position. With the ball at the Seattle Seahawks' 29-yard line, quarterback Case Keenum called a new play. It would be a pass. Phillip's mind raced as he quickly remembered what he was supposed to do and where he was supposed to go.

The football was snapped, and Phillip sprinted toward the left sideline. When he turned to look back at Keenum, the quarterback was already tossing him the ball.

Without stopping, Phillip cradled it into his stomach and then spun forward. There was no one in front of him for 20 yards. The field between him and the end zone was almost completely open. Phillip turned on the speed. The only defender with a chance to stop him was blocked out of his way. Behind him, another defender dove at Phillip's feet in desperation. The running back kicked up his leg and zoomed into the end zone.

Touchdown!

In his very first National Football League (NFL) game, Phillip Lindsay had scored the Denver Broncos' very first touchdown of the season. It was a dream come true for the rookie who had grown up cheering for the orange and blue.

This was only the beginning. Things were going to get even better.

Phillip totaled 102 yards from scrimmage in his first NFL game.

1

STAR SIBLINGS

Phillip Lindsay was born in Denver, Colorado, on July 24, 1994. The summer baby was the third child of Troy and Diane Lindsay. Sparkle was Phillip's 9-year-old sister, and Cheri was 5.

Phillip grew up in Aurora, Colorado, just east of the Denver metropolitan area. His parents were respected in their community. Mr. Lindsay worked as a city bus driver. Mrs. Lindsay was a psychotherapist, helping people with mental illnesses and emotional difficulties. They were honest, hardworking parents, but they sometimes struggled financially. They couldn't afford a good house in a nice location. Instead, their family lived in a 4-bedroom home in a neighborhood that wasn't always safe. The high-crime area meant that Mr. and Mrs. Lindsay needed to work even harder to protect their children and to keep them out of trouble.

Health issues added an additional layer of struggles for Mrs. Lindsay. She suffered from dermatomyositis, an inflammatory disease that affected her muscles and skin. It flared up after Phillip was born, and the painful condition sometimes brought her to tears. But Mrs. Lindsay never let it bring her down. She remained a devoted, loving mother on even the worst of days.

Phillip was an active, energetic child. He was constantly in motion. Even as a baby, while other kids his age would crawl, that method wasn't fast enough for Phillip. Instead, he quickly scooted around on his hands and feet.

That hustle fit right in at the Lindsay household. The family was sports-focused. Sports were a part of Phillip's everyday life. Sparkle and Cheri excelled in basketball and volleyball, and Phillip attended all of their games.

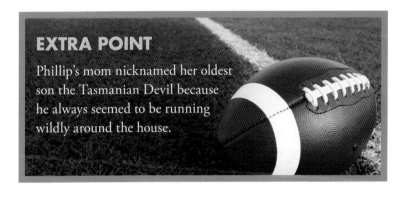

EXTRA POINT

Phillip's mom nicknamed her oldest son the Tasmanian Devil because he always seemed to be running wildly around the house.

A year after Phillip was born, the Lindsays' home grew even busier. His younger brother Zachary joined the family. The Lindsays' youngest child, Marcus, was born when Phillip was 4. Zachary and Marcus would grow to become football players in high school and in college. That wasn't surprising, considering their dad's past.

Mr. Lindsay had played high school football for 3 years at Thomas Jefferson High School in Denver. Back in the late 1970s, he was a star running back, and he wasn't just good— he was great. In his high school career, Mr. Lindsay had rushed for 4,400 yards—a Denver Public Schools record! He went on to play in college at Colorado State University.

Sandwiched between pairs of exceptionally talented siblings, Phillip seemed destined for greatness. But talent alone wasn't enough for the Lindsay children. They worked tirelessly to improve their skills, and they poured every ounce of energy into the games they loved. Phillip saw this in his sisters, and they became role models for him. Sparkle and Cheri taught him how important hard work was for success. They showed him that setting goals was only the first step; he needed to earn his rewards through determination and perseverance. Those were lessons that Phillip would never forget, and they would ultimately change his life.

Not everything was perfect between Phillip and his sisters, though. They liked to pick on him. Cheri, in particular, would sometimes bully her little brother. Phillip typically ended up crying and running off to tell on his sisters.

Despite those occasional rough moments, the Lindsay children loved each other, and they enjoyed their share of fun. They didn't often get to see their classmates outside of school, so the 5 siblings became best friends. They would play catch and shoot hoops together. They imagined themselves as "cops and robbers" in the backyard.

EXTRA POINT

One of Phillip's favorite things to do was dress up in costumes and pretend to be popular movie characters and superheroes.

Phillip also enjoyed going to his sisters' games. Those were family events, and everyone went along to cheer and offer support. By the time he was in kindergarten, Phillip was regularly attending Sparkle's high school games.

By the second grade, he began playing a sport of his own: football.

2

Phillip joined organized football when he was only 8 years old. He played with 9- and 10-year-olds, but he knew that he would do well because he had an excellent coach: his father.

Even though Phillip was among the smallest in the league, he started out on the offensive line. He wanted to run the ball and score touchdowns, but he always did his best wherever he played. He bravely learned to block opponents much bigger than he was. He performed so well that, despite playing with older children, he was given an award for Most Valuable Player.

Over the next 3 years, Phillip continued to develop as one of the best players in his age group. He earned his chance at running back—and more. He also excelled at wide receiver and became a tenacious tackler on defense. The place where he shined brightest, though, was on special teams. He thrilled parents, coaches, and teammates with his exciting runbacks on kickoffs. He returned several kickoffs for touchdowns.

When he wasn't playing football, Phillip watched it on television. His family rooted for the Denver Broncos, and Phillip dreamed of attending a game. Unfortunately, the Lindsays could never afford to go. But Phillip owned a Broncos jersey. He proudly wore Quentin Griffin's number 22—which had also been Mr. Lindsay's jersey number in high school. Griffin played for the Broncos in 2003 and 2004, until a knee injury cut his season (and ultimately his career) short. Like Phillip, Griffin had been small for a running back: 5 feet, 7 inches tall and 198 pounds.

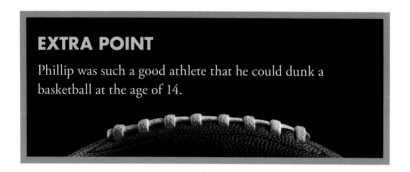

EXTRA POINT

Phillip was such a good athlete that he could dunk a basketball at the age of 14.

By 2008, Phillip had solidified himself at the running back position. The 14-year-old wasn't just the best back in his eighth-grade class—he looked good enough to play at the high school level.

But the future of high school football in Denver was something of a question. The number of students who participated in the sport was low; some of the district's schools struggled to find enough players for a team. Because of that, Denver Public Schools (DPS) was largely considered the worst football league in Colorado. Rumors began to swirl that DPS might cut football across the entire district.

Desperate for a solution, DPS turned to Denver's professional football team, the Broncos, for help. The district proposed a "Futures" football program for the city's seventh and eighth graders, and Broncos Charities eagerly agreed to fund it.

The goal of this new program was to give middle-schoolers an exciting new football opportunity—an incentive for participating in the sport. More importantly, it would provide a chance for players to improve their football skills and to learn valuable life lessons in a positive, focused environment.

Futures Football held its first event in the spring of 2009. Phillip was among the students who participated. He and his middle-school teammates were given new uniforms and new football equipment. They also had an opportunity to meet a few Denver Broncos players.

EXTRA POINT

Phillip received an autograph from Broncos wide receiver Demaryius Thomas in 2009. Nine years later, the two would become teammates.

The Denver Broncos were essential to the success of Futures Football.

The eighth graders on Phillip's team were just a few months away from becoming freshmen at Denver South High School. They received the added benefit of practicing and playing football under the guidance of South's head football coach. Phillip was already well acquainted with his new coach. It was his father's brother—and Phillip's uncle—Tony Lindsay.

South High School's varsity football team, like the rest of the league, would need to make great strides to become competitive. Coach Lindsay saw plenty of potential in his Futures Football team. He took full advantage of his time working with the young players, and in his mind, he hatched an incredible plan for the future.

3

FRESHMAN SUCCESS

Mr. and Mrs. Lindsay understood the importance of a college education. Those who graduated from college typically found better jobs and had more opportunities than those who did not. The Lindsays also knew that—with 5 children and with college tuition costing many thousands of dollars per year—their family could not afford it.

Mr. and Mrs. Lindsay told their children that they would have 2 options: get multiple jobs and work their way through college or get a sports scholarship so that college tuition was free.

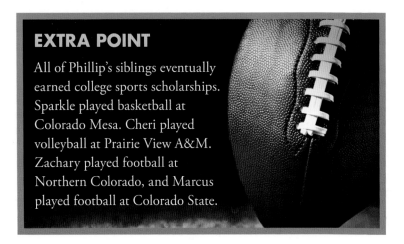

EXTRA POINT

All of Phillip's siblings eventually earned college sports scholarships. Sparkle played basketball at Colorado Mesa. Cheri played volleyball at Prairie View A&M. Zachary played football at Northern Colorado, and Marcus played football at Colorado State.

Denver South High School

Phillip had yet to play a down of high school football, but he believed in his talent. He planned on getting a scholarship to play college football.

That didn't mean he could take it easy in the classroom. His parents expected Phillip—and all of the Lindsay children—to be above-average students. A "C" grade wasn't good enough. Mr. and Mrs. Lindsay would only accept "A" and "B" grades. Every day, they watched their children do their homework to make sure that it got done.

For Phillip, schoolwork was an especially difficult challenge. He had a learning disability. Many everyday tasks that were easy for other students—such as writing and taking notes—were extremely difficult for Phillip. Luckily, he was able to get extra help, both at home and at school, and he met the academic standards that his parents set.

On the field, Phillip set another goal for himself: He intended to break his dad's rushing record. His uncle/ coach had plans to help him achieve that.

Coach Lindsay knew how to turn South High School's subpar Rebels football squad into one of the state's best teams. It wouldn't happen quickly, and it might take a few years to get there—but Coach Lindsay was going to do something that teams around the country didn't often do: He was going to play his freshmen. He believed that experience against bigger, stronger, older opponents would help his youngest players get better. In 3 years, when those freshmen were seniors, they would be tough to beat.

He hatched his plan against the Golden Demons on September 3, 2009. Phillip wore his dad's old football number, 22, in honor of his father—and he wore it well. Phillip ran wild, gaining 175 yards on 15 carries, including a 74-yard touchdown dash. He added a 9-yard touchdown reception to his day. He appeared to be the best player on the field, despite being one of the youngest. However, the Demons completed 5 touchdown passes on their way to a 47–33 victory.

South High School also dropped their second game of the season. But in Week 3, Phillip again exploded on offense. This time, he rushed for 157 yards and scored 2 touchdowns versus Green Mountain, leading his team to their first win, 28–0.

The Rebels' success continued as they blew out their next 3 opponents, 44–8, 47–6, and 60–6. Phillip rushed for more than 140 yards and at least 2 touchdowns in each of those contests.

South High School split its final 4 games, but their most dominating win came against Denver North on October 23. The Rebels outscored their city rival, 55–0, and Phillip posted his highest rushing total of the year: 178 yards.

Phillip's team finished with a respectable 6–4 record. Phillip impressed football fans across the state with his surprising season. All told, he rushed for 1,265 yards and 13 touchdowns, along with 10 receptions for 169 yards and 2 receiving touchdowns. As a linebacker on defense, Phillip recorded 74 tackles, 4 sacks, 1 interception, and 1 fumble recovery. He was named to the West Metro All-Conference first-team on offense and second-team on defense.

The rest of the DPS league took notice. They would need to contend with the star running back and his young team for 3 more years.

EXTRA POINT

Phillip also played on the varsity basketball team as a freshman. He lettered as a guard.

4

⚞⚞⚞ WINNING SEASONS ⚞⚞⚞

On the football field, Phillip was a standout player. Off the field, he was just like other kids his age. He loved to hang out, especially with his brothers. He played video games and held an interest in martial arts. He enjoyed exploring area trails on his mountain bike, an activity that he often shared with his dad.

"Pops," as the children called Mr. Lindsay, oversaw Phillip's training throughout the year. They ran football drills together and watched film. Sometimes Phillip even watched tapes of his dad's old games. It was all to help Phillip improve upon his 2009 performance.

With Phillip leading the rushing attack, the Rebels hoped to be more successful in 2010. In their opening game of the season, South started quickly, putting up 22 points in the first half. Phillip contributed in all phases of the game. He ran the ball, caught the ball, returned kickoffs and punts, and made tackles on defense.

The Golden Demons held the Rebels scoreless in the second half, though. They rallied to defeat South High School, 26–22. Phillip finished with 164 all-purpose yards and a rushing touchdown. His day was highlighted by a 44-yard punt return.

It was a disappointing outcome, but the team recovered quickly. They rattled off 3 straight wins in their next 3 games.

Phillip's first 100-yard rushing game of the season came against Denver East on October 2. He exploded for 142 yards on just 15 carries. But the Rebels saw their winning streak snapped. They fell to the Angels, 26–13.

Once again, South High School bounced back from a loss. This time, it was against the 5–0 Lakewood Tigers. Phillip sparked his team in one of the most thrilling offensive battles of the year. The all-purpose sophomore scored on an 82-yard kickoff return, and he caught touchdown passes of 22 yards and 16 yards. Phillip also added 138 yards rushing, including a 40-yard touchdown run. His 272 total yards and 4 total touchdowns lifted the Rebels to victory, 41–34.

A week later, Phillip caught fire against the Lincoln Lancers. He tallied 17 carries for 250 yards, and he added 2 touchdowns. The Rebels trounced the Lancers, 48–0.

South notched 2 more victories to finish their regular season on a 4-game winning streak. In those 2 games, Phillip ran for 302 yards and an incredible 6 touchdowns.

The 7–2 record qualified the Rebels for the Colorado High School Activities Association 5A football playoffs. They matched up against the 6–3 Arapahoe Warriors.

South zipped to an early lead, scoring 21 points in the first quarter. But the offense fizzled after that, and the defense couldn't stop the Warriors' rushing attack. All

together, Arapahoe ran for 309 yards and 5 touchdowns, en route to a 56–28 victory.

The loss ended a stellar season for the Rebels and for Phillip. He finished with 164 rushes for 1,261 yards and scored 22 touchdowns.

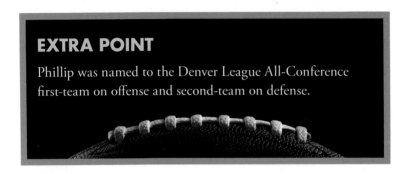

EXTRA POINT

Phillip was named to the Denver League All-Conference first-team on offense and second-team on defense.

His junior year began with a rugged defensive battle against Golden. The Demons led, 6–0, for most of the game, but the Rebels scored their only touchdown in the fourth quarter. They came away with an 8–6 victory.

The following week, Phillip broke loose for 206 yards, but his team fell to Poudre, 23–20.

South reeled off 2 straight blowout wins before getting dominated by Lakewood, 42–0. Early in October, the team's record stood at 3–3.

Desperate to turn the mediocre start into a memorable season, Phillip took over. The following week, he put together one of the finest games of his high school career. Against the Lincoln Lancers, he carried the ball 17 times and rushed for an eye-popping 300 yards—his highest total ever. He added 4 rushing touchdowns in the game. He also intercepted a pass on the defensive side of the ball and returned it 39 yards for a touchdown. The Rebels scored 42 points in the first half and won, 64–13.

Phillip followed that performance with 231 yards rushing against Niwot and 225 yards rushing versus George Washington High School in Denver. Both games resulted in easy wins for South, lifting them to a record of 6–3.

That was good enough to earn a playoff berth, and their first matchup pitted them against the Bear Creek Bears. Both teams came into the game with similar records, but the Bears were favored to win. Phillip again carried the load, rushing for 170 yards, but his Rebels fell short. They lost, 35–20, putting an end to their 2011 season.

Phillip was once again named to the Denver League All-Conference first-team on offense. He also made the first-team on defense. More impressively, he was named to the All-State first-team by *The Denver Post*.

Phillip's 1,762 rushing yards brought his career total to 4,288 yards. He was just over 100 yards behind his father's rushing record, and he still had his entire senior season to go. The record would surely be his.

5

BROKEN DREAMS

After the season, Phillip began to focus on college. He loved his state, and he was proud to be a Coloradan. He also wanted to stay close to his family. Multiple area colleges were interested in Phillip, and he was tempted to follow in his father's footsteps to Colorado State University. He also had a chance to attend Boise State, in Idaho, a college known for its outstanding football program. But Phillip decided to play for the Buffaloes at the University of Colorado (CU) in Boulder, just an hour from home.

On March 22, 2012, Phillip became the year's first junior to commit to Colorado. It was a special day for the Lindsay family, worthy of celebration. But the happy day quickly turned sour. The family returned home to find that they had been robbed. Burglars had broken in through a basement window and had stolen the family's valuable possessions—including Mrs. Lindsay's precious jewelry.

If that weren't bad enough, the criminals used a stick to beat the Lindsays' family dog, a German Shepard mix named Rambo.

Fortunately, Rambo made a full recovery, and the crooks were later arrested. But Mrs. Lindsay's jewelry was nowhere to be found. For months, Phillip searched all the local pawn shops and thrift stores, but he was never able to find his mom's stolen belongings.

In the spring, Phillip joined the Rebels' track-and-field team. His speed made him an excellent sprinter. He ran the 100-meter dash, 200-meter dash, and 400-meter dash, along with relay races in which 4 team members each ran part of the race.

His first love was football, though, and heading into his senior season, he was getting noticed. Phillip was selected to the MaxPreps 2012 Colorado Preseason All-State Team and to *SuperPrep* magazine's All-Midlands team.

South High School, now in Class 4A, was getting the recognition it deserved too. Coach Lindsay's plan to play his freshmen back in 2009 had paid off. Those players, now seniors, made the Rebels a top-10-ranked team in the state.

Phillip's senior season kicked off on August 31, 2012. The running back had just 2 things on his mind: win the game and break his father's rushing record. He succeeded on both counts. Phillip ran for 160 yards on 22 carries and scored a touchdown, helping South defeat the Mesa Ridge Grizzlies, 42–34.

The news wasn't all good coming out of the game, though. The day that Phillip had been waiting to celebrate since he first picked up a football took an unexpected turn. Just minutes after breaking his father's record, Phillip grabbed a handoff, cut hard off his left leg, and heard a series of popping sounds in his knee.

Phillip tried to keep running, but his leg would no longer cooperate. He fell to the ground, his knee throbbing. The pain seemed to come mostly from behind his knee, so he was diagnosed with a hamstring injury.

The injury forced Phillip to sit out the following week against Poudre. The rest provided a chance for his hamstring to heal. Even without their star runner, the powerful Rebels team dominated the competition, winning 52–0 in a game that was never in doubt.

Another week later, Phillip's knee was still sore, but it was an injury that he believed he could play through. He suited up for the rivalry matchup against Denver East.

The senior star tried to gut it out, but he wasn't able to finish the first half. Still, he carried the ball 9 times and managed to gain 139 yards rushing, including a 66-yard touchdown. For the first time in Phillip's career, his team beat the Angels, 53–34.

However, the injury seemed to worsen with every step. Phillip's knee was checked again on Tuesday, September 18. This time, he was given a magnetic resonance imaging (MRI) scan, which allowed doctors to see inside his knee. The news was worse—the worst that Phillip could have imagined. It wasn't just a minor hamstring injury. Phillip had torn his anterior cruciate ligament (ACL). This injury would require surgery—and, just like that, his football career at South High School was over.

Suddenly, Phillip's future was in question. Football was supposed to be his ticket out of the neighborhood. It was his path to a college education and a chance to become whatever he wanted to be. Without a football scholarship, Phillip didn't know if he could afford college—and with such a serious knee injury, he didn't know if he would ever be able to play again.

In one terrible moment, Phillip had lost the game that he loved and the life that he had dreamed about since he was 8 years old.

To make matters worse, Phillip's future team, the Colorado Buffaloes, finished their season with a 1–11 record. The university fired head coach Jon Embree, the man who had offered Phillip a scholarship.

The new coach, Mike MacIntyre, didn't know Phillip and had never seen him play. It seemed unlikely, then, that Coach MacIntyre would give a scholarship to a stranger who couldn't walk without crutches, let alone run.

It was enough to sink even an optimistic, positive spirit like Phillip into a state of depression.

A torn anterior cruciate ligament (ACL)

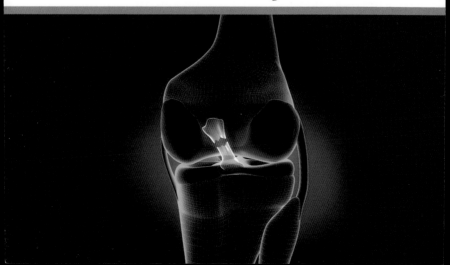

6

❧❧❧❧❧❧ INSPIRATIONS ❧❧❧❧❧❧❧

The day after his MRI, Phillip's knee was operated on. Then the long and painful rehabilitation process began. Those first few days were especially difficult. Phillip continued to wonder and continued to worry about his future. He was in desperate need of something—anything—that could provide a glimmer of hope.

On Saturday, September 23, the telephone rang.

Phillip was at home, watching the Colorado Buffaloes' afternoon football game on TV. When he took the call, he couldn't have been more surprised. The caller was someone whom Phillip had never met and had never spoken to before. It was the Denver Broncos' star running back, Willis McGahee.

McGahee had heard about Phillip's misfortune and understood it as well as anyone could. In 2003, McGahee had been a star at the University of Miami. His college career ended in the Fiesta Bowl National Championship Game, when he tore 3 ligaments in his knee, including his ACL. McGahee had eventually made a full recovery and was now in the midst of a successful football career.

He offered Phillip some words of encouragement and assured the high school senior that he, too, could make a full recovery. It wouldn't be easy, but it could be done.

For Phillip, the phone call was exactly what he needed. The time for feeling sad, upset, sorry—that was over. It was time to get back to work.

The phone call itself wasn't enough, though. Phillip would need the aid of his entire family. He couldn't bend or straighten his knee, but that was the first step on the path to recovery. So his dad had to sit on Phillip's back while the rest of the family pushed his leg, working to get the knee moving again. It caused so much pain that Phillip would scream, and the entire family would cry.

Those were challenging moments, but his family members worked together to keep his spirits high. Phillip found the extra motivation that he needed from his mother. Her dermatomyositis symptoms worsened, and she was in pain every day. She began losing hair, and sometimes her feet were numb. There were days when it was a struggle for her to walk. Yet she continued living her life without complaint, setting an example of strength and perseverance for Phillip and the rest of her family.

Phillip's mood and his physical health continued to improve. He soon heard from the University of Colorado. Coach MacIntyre had been told by a number of high school coaches that Phillip was worth keeping. The coach met with Phillip and saw a short, skinny kid who couldn't bend his knee. He didn't know if Phillip would ever play again, but he also sensed an inner strength and a positive energy within the 18-year old. He told Phillip that he would honor Coach Embree's scholarship offer—so Phillip's future plans were back on course.

Physical therapy became a daily part of Phillip's life. He exercised his knee, determined to get it back into shape. Just a few of weeks after his surgery, Phillip was able to walk without his crutches.

On the football field, South High School missed Phillip, but they were well balanced. Phillip cheered from the sidelines, and the team was able to thrive without him. The Rebels went on to an unbelievable 9–1 regular season, and they rolled through the playoffs—all the way to the state championship game.

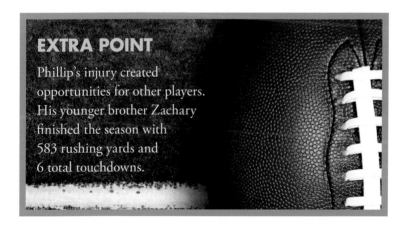

EXTRA POINT

Phillip's injury created opportunities for other players. His younger brother Zachary finished the season with 583 rushing yards and 6 total touchdowns.

The Monarch Coyotes edged South High School, 17–14, but the Rebels' run was a tremendous accomplishment—for the school and for the Denver Public Schools league. It had risen to prominence in just 4 years, thanks in large part to Futures Football and to players like Phillip.

Even though he had played in just 2 games, Phillip received recognition from *PrepStar* as an All-Central Region running back. He finished his high school career with 545 rushing attempts for 4,587 yards (an 8.4-yard average per carry). He tallied 5,747 all-purpose yards and 57 total touchdowns. He was South's all-time leader in rushing yards and all-purpose yards.

7

A NEW BUFFALO

Phillip was a highly regarded college prospect. He was considered to be a 3-star recruit (out of a possible 5 stars). That put him in the top 1% of all high school seniors, and he ranked among the top 100 running backs in the country. *The Denver Post* listed him as the best running back prospect in Colorado and the fifth best Colorado prospect overall.

Given his high ratings, he perhaps could have looked at more successful college football programs. He could have chosen a team that provided more opportunities to win—and more chances to get noticed nationally. The Buffaloes had finished the 2012 season in last place in the South Division of the Pac-12 Conference. Their 1–11 record was the worst in the team's history. It hadn't simply been one unlucky year, either. Colorado's recent history was less than stellar. The team hadn't qualified for a post-season bowl game since 2007.

Yet Phillip was fiercely loyal to those who stood by him. He would always remember Coach MacIntyre and the university for sticking with him after his injury. Plus, he relished the challenge of helping to turn the local team into a winner. There was no chance that he would abandon them and go somewhere else.

National Signing Day came on February 6, 2013. It was a day in which a commitment to a college became official. On that day, players could sign a National Letter of Intent (NLI)—a legal agreement between the player and the school of choice. It stated that the college would provide the student with an athletic scholarship and that the student would play for their team.

Phillip proudly signed his NLI on that day, officially making him a Colorado Buffalo.

EXTRA POINT

Phillip became the first South High School Rebel to join CU's football team since 1983.

He finished out the remainder of the school year. He graduated from high school with a 3.49 grade point average, missing the honor roll by 0.01 point.

His summer at home was short. Freshmen football players reported to college in July. His parents drove him to Boulder, and his family helped him get moved into his new college apartment.

It was an emotional time. Phillip would miss seeing his parents and brothers every day. He would miss being

The University of Colorado Boulder

there for his mom, helping her with everything from the laundry to putting on her shoes. He would need to adjust to living on his own, without his mom and dad to guide him, for the first time in his life.

At the same time, he was proud of himself for being there. He was independent now, able to begin carving out his own life. He was living his dream of playing football in college.

But he couldn't play yet. His knee wasn't ready. He still needed time to get it back to 100%. Because of this, the coaches gave Phillip a "redshirt" designation for the year. Athletes were allowed to play college football for 4 years.

"Redshirting" a player meant that he could practice with the team but couldn't play in any games. A "redshirt" year didn't count against the player's 4 years of college eligibility. Phillip would be able to get healthy and learn during the 2013 season, and he still had 4 years to play! He took full advantage of his extra season.

His new teammates were some of the best players that Phillip had ever seen. So he needed to make himself stronger and faster than he already was. He exercised relentlessly, impressing everyone with his work ethic.

He spent the fall season practicing at running back. He also filled in with the scout team, which helped the Buffaloes prepare for each game. During practice, the scout team pretended to be Colorado's next opponent, running that team's plays and competing against Colorado's starters and key players.

Phillip took it upon himself to be the best scout team player that he could. He felt that the harder he worked, the better it made his team's defense. The coaching staff noticed. At the end of the season, Phillip was awarded the Offensive Scout Player of the Year.

EXTRA POINT

The Buffaloes finished the 2013 season with a record of 4–8, three wins better than the previous year.

8

Everything clicked for Phillip on the football field, but that wasn't the case in the classroom. Phillip was in a new environment—without the educational support that had helped him in high school. His learning disability began to create problems again.

Coaches and academic advisors were there to help, but Phillip refused to ask for it. He didn't want anyone else to know about his difficulties. Instead, he tried to cope on his own—and he wasn't doing well. Phillip was failing some of his classes and barely passing others.

His mom and dad were far more concerned with his educational progress than with his accomplishments on the football field. They called Phillip every day, and every day they asked how his classes were going. Phillip confided in them about his problems—and those problems continued to worsen.

Eventually, Mrs. Lindsay had heard enough. She decided that, if her son wouldn't ask for help, she would do it for him. She called his academic advisors and explained Phillip's situation. They, in turn, spoke with Phillip, and he finally asked for the assistance that he needed.

Phillip was paired with a learning specialist named Michelle Brannigan, an associate director of the Herbst Academic Center. She worked with Phillip on everything from studying techniques to test-taking skills. Over time, Phillip began to improve. He realized that studies and sports shared a lot in common. Both required hard work, dedication, and perseverance.

Phillip began to focus on getting his homework done during the week—before each Friday. That way, during the weekends, he could concentrate entirely on football.

The new strategies worked. Phillip's grades improved, and his college education got back on track. Perhaps more importantly, he learned that it was okay to ask for help. With his academics under control, Phillip could prepare for the 2014 football season.

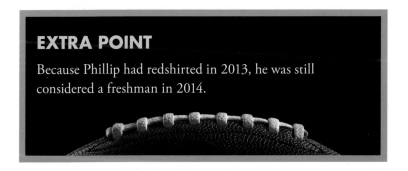

EXTRA POINT

Because Phillip had redshirted in 2013, he was still considered a freshman in 2014.

Phillip set his sights on Friday, August 29. It was the date of the Buffaloes' first game—and Phillip's first official game in nearly 2 years. CU's opponent would be Colorado State, the alma mater of Phillip's father.

Phillip didn't start the game at running back, but he was in the mix for playing time. He carried the ball twice but netted 0 yards rushing. He did start as the primary kickoff returner. He ran back 2 kicks for 43 yards.

Overall, this Rocky Mountain Showdown belonged to the Rams. They defeated the Buffaloes, 31–17.

Colorado won 2 of its next 3 games to even the record at 2–2. But then the slide began. While Phillip continued to see a handful of opportunities, both rushing and returning kicks, the Buffaloes dropped their final 8 games.

Phillip's best performance came on November 8, in Arizona against the Wildcats. He led Colorado's rushing attack with 17 attempts for 115 yards, including his longest run of the season: 36 yards. The Buffaloes kept the score close for much of the game; they trailed by just 4 points after 3 quarters. But the Wildcats eventually pulled away and won, 38–20.

Colorado finished with a 2–10 record, but Phillip was a bright spot. Against Oregon on November 22, he racked up 49 rushing yards, 26 receiving yards, and 142 kickoff return yards. The total of 217 all-purpose yards was a single-game record for CU redshirt freshmen.

He ended the season with 1,358 all-purpose yards, a new CU freshman record. Part of that total included 849 yards on kickoff returns—the third most in school history. Rounding out his all-purpose total, Phillip had 79 carries for 391 yards, and 14 receptions for 118 yards.

EXTRA POINT

During spring football practices, Phillip was honored with the Fred Casotti Award, given to the most improved Colorado offensive back.

9

╼╼╼╼╼╼ FEATURED BACK ╼╼╼╼╼╼

Phillip remained close to his family. He spoke with his parents every day. He played video games like *Call of Duty* online with his siblings. He scouted the area's bike trails to share with his dad when he visited. Their rides together were a special time. Phillip used those quiet, private opportunities to talk to his father about whatever was on his mind. Good news, bad news, secrets, Phillip told his dad everything.

The news was good heading into Phillip's sophomore season. He was a top player on special teams—selected to the preseason All-Pac-12 second team as a kickoff returner by *Phil Steele's College Football*. He was also battling with 3 other players for a starting job on offense.

His enthusiasm, toughness, loyalty, and work ethic had won over his coaches and teammates. He was among 12 players chosen for the team's leadership council, which made him a team captain.

The Buffaloes dropped their first game of the 2015 season in Hawaii, 28–20. Their next opponent was the Massachusetts Minutemen. Late in the second quarter, Colorado advanced the football down to the 2-yard line. Phillip lined up deep in the backfield. When the ball was snapped, he charged forward. The quarterback spun and extended the ball. Phillip grabbed it and sliced straight ahead, through an opening in the line. A defender met him at the 1-yard line, but Phillip lowered his shoulder and plowed through him. Phillip scored the first touchdown of his college career, giving his team a 30–14 lead! Colorado trounced Massachusetts by a final score of 48–14.

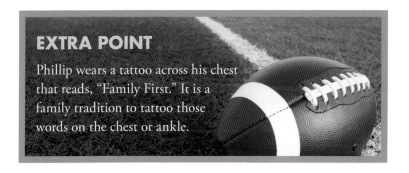

EXTRA POINT

Phillip wears a tattoo across his chest that reads, "Family First." It is a family tradition to tattoo those words on the chest or ankle.

That led into a matchup against the rival Colorado State Rams in Denver's Sports Authority Field at Mile High on Saturday, September 19. The Rams jumped to an early lead, scoring 2 touchdowns in the first quarter. The Buffaloes responded with 10 points in the second. The teams traded scores in the third and fourth quarters, and the opponents finished regulation tied at 24. In overtime, Colorado blocked a Rams' field goal and then kicked a field goal of their own to come away with a 27–24 win.

Leading rusher Michael Adkins exited the game early with an injury, yet Phillip wasn't much of a factor in the victory. He finished the day with 8 rushes for 22 yards.

However, with Adkins still out a week later, Phillip became the featured back. He played his best game of the season. In the Buffaloes' 48–0 trouncing of Nicholls State University, Phillip rushed for a season-high 113 yards and scored 2 touchdowns.

At 3–1, Colorado was off to a promising start. But the streaky team lost their next 3 games. Phillip continued to pace them on the ground, but the offense struggled to keep up with the likes of Pac-12 rivals Oregon, Arizona State, and Arizona.

On October 24, the Buffaloes visited Corvallis, Oregon, to play the Oregon State Beavers. Both defenses dominated the day, as neither team could find a rhythm on offense. Colorado quarterback Sefo Liufau scored on a 4-yard touchdown run early in the fourth quarter, and that proved to be the difference. The Buffaloes went home with a 17–13 victory.

Unfortunately, it would be their last. Colorado went 0–5 to finish out another disappointing season.

Phillip made great strides in his sophomore year. He started 6 of the team's 13 games, and he was Colorado's leading rusher with 140 attempts that went for 653 yards and 6 touchdowns. He also added 26 receptions for 211 yards and a receiving touchdown.

He was honored with the Derek Singleton Award, given to the Colorado player who best demonstrated spirit, dedication, and enthusiasm. He was also given the

Hammer Award for the hardest legal hit of the year and the Dick Anderson Award for outstanding toughness.

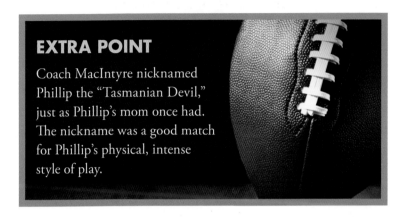

EXTRA POINT

Coach MacIntyre nicknamed Phillip the "Tasmanian Devil," just as Phillip's mom once had. The nickname was a good match for Phillip's physical, intense style of play.

Life was about more than just football for Phillip, though. He saw his "football player" status as a way to affect people's lives and to make the world a better place. To that end, he began visiting elementary schools in Aurora, Boulder, and Denver. He shared inspirational messages about being a good student and helping others.

10

WINNING GAMES

A combined 6 wins in Phillip's first 2 seasons on the field wasn't good enough for him. He felt frustrated, and he believed that he and his team could do better. That frustration bubbled over the following summer.

There was a general lack of focus on the team. Some players arrived late to events. Others skipped workouts. A team meeting was called, and Phillip—once again a team captain—took charge. He emotionally called upon the players to come together, work harder, and commit to the season ahead.

His teammates demonstrated their respect for the young leader by doing exactly as he asked. The levels of intensity and effort dramatically improved, and it suddenly seemed possible that a tremendous season lay ahead.

In early September, the Buffaloes walloped their first 2 opponents by a combined score of 100–14. However, CU next dropped a tough road game against the Michigan Wolverines before jumping into their Pac-12 schedule. Their first matchup pitted them against the Oregon Ducks.

Phillip gave Colorado the lead in the first quarter, capping an 80-yard drive with a 1-yard touchdown run. The Buffaloes added 2 field goals, while Oregon put a touchdown of their own on the board. After the first quarter, Colorado led, 16–7.

Three minutes into the second quarter, a thrilling 61-yard pass play set up another Buffaloes' touchdown. With the score at 23–7, it appeared that a rout was on. But the Ducks answered with 10 straight points. Colorado squeezed in one more field goal as time expired, and the Buffaloes led at halftime, 26–17.

Colorado began the second half with a 48-yard touchdown pass from Steven Montez to Devin Ross. But the rest of the third quarter was all Ducks. They reeled off 3 straight touchdowns and rallied to a 38–33 lead.

Midway through the fourth quarter, Buffalo strung together a 7-play, 70-yard touchdown drive to retake the lead. Oregon responded with an 8-play, 51-yard drive all the way to Colorado's 7-yard line. Defensive back Ahkello Witherspoon intercepted a pass in the end zone to preserve the Buffaloes' lead—and the victory, 41–38.

Colorado followed that win with a 47–6 thrashing of Oregon State before falling short against the University of Southern California, 21–17. In the loss, Phillip caught 6 passes for 105 yards, including a 67-yard touchdown pass from receiver Bryce Bobo on a trick play.

A week later, Arizona State visited Folsom Field in Boulder. With 4:47 left in the half, Phillip took a handoff from Arizona State's 13-yard line. He darted through the open hole and then cut to his right toward open space. At the 5-yard line, 2 defenders trapped him. Phillip cut to

An entrance to Colorado's Folsom Field

his left and side-stepped the first. Then he turned that cut into a spin move that caused the second defender to run past him. A third defender caught Phillip and grabbed his legs. Phillip fell forward, landed on the second defender, and scooted forward on the defender's back until the ball crossed the goal line! The score gave Colorado a 23–10 lead, and the Buffaloes never looked back.

Colorado began the third-quarter at their 25-yard line. When the ball was snapped, the quarterback handed the ball to Phillip. The running back burst through the left side of the line. Ten yards downfield, 2 defenders tried to grab him, but Phillip jetted between them. He didn't stop until 75 yards later when he crossed the goal line.

Phillip added a 4-yard touchdown run in the fourth to close out the game. All together, Phillip carried the football 26 times and accumulated 219 yards rushing and 3 touchdowns.

He was named the Pac-12's Offensive Player of the Week for his excellent game. He also won CU's award for Athlete of the Week. He gave his offensive linemen all the credit for his successful game.

The 40–16 victory ignited the Buffaloes on a 6-game winning streak. Phillip rushed for a team-high 741 yards during that stretch of time, leading Colorado to the Pac-12 Championship game against the Washington Huskies on December 2.

Sadly, that contest didn't go the Buffaloes' way. Phillip scored a touchdown on a 3-yard run late in the first quarter, but Colorado's highlights ended there. Washington put 31 points on the board before CU scored again. The Huskies claimed the conference championship by a final margin of 41–10.

Still, Colorado's impressive 10–3 season was more than enough to qualify them for an appearance in a bowl game—the team's first in 9 years. The Buffaloes were invited to San Antonio, Texas, to play against the Oklahoma State University Cowboys in the Valero Alamo Bowl on December 29.

The Buffaloes fell, 38–8, but the disappointing finale couldn't diminish their successful season. During their run, Colorado was ranked as high as the ninth best team in the country, and they finished at number 17.

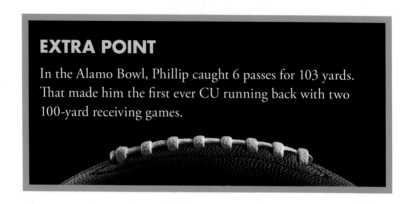

EXTRA POINT

In the Alamo Bowl, Phillip caught 6 passes for 103 yards. That made him the first ever CU running back with two 100-yard receiving games.

Phillip totaled 1,189 yards rushing, and he led the Pac-12 with 16 rushing touchdowns. He set a record for Colorado running backs with 47 receptions, and he added 390 receiving yards and a receiving touchdown. He was named to the All-Pac-12 second team, and he was selected to the All-Colorado Team by the Colorado Chapter of the National Football Foundation and College Hall of Fame.

His team honored him with the John Mack Award for most outstanding offensive player. He also won the Derek Singleton award for spirit, dedication, and enthusiasm, as well as the team award for Best Interview.

In the spring of his junior year, Phillip was 1 of only 4 student-athletes in the entire university selected to receive the Ceal Berry Leadership Award. The honor was in recognition of inspiring teammates, the campus, and the community.

11

RECORD BREAKER

Heading into his final season for CU, Phillip was again selected as a team captain. It made him 1 of only 3 Buffaloes ever to act as a captain for 3 years. Expectations were high for the star running back. He was garnering attention as one of the best rushers in the Pac-12—and even as a top performer in the country.

He backed up that buzz in CU's opening game: the 2017 Rocky Mountain Showdown against Colorado State. Phillip kicked off the scoring midway through the first quarter when he ran in a touchdown from 45 yards out. It was the highlight of a day in which he rushed for 144 yards on 19 attempts, sparking a 17–3 victory.

A week later, Phillip rushed for 87 yards and scored another touchdown, as Colorado defeated the Texas State Bobcats, 37–3.

On September 16, the Northern Colorado Bears visited Folsom Field—a game that was extra special for Phillip and his family. Phillip's younger brother Zachary was a reserve running back on the Bears' team. The brothers competed against each other on the football field for the very first time.

The day belonged to Phillip. He carried the football 26 times and rushed for 152 yards, including a 5-yard touchdown in the first quarter—a score that gave CU the lead for good. His Buffaloes won, 41–21.

EXTRA POINT

Zachary ran the football once for 5 yards in the loss.

Colorado's promising 3–0 start was followed by 2 losses against Pac-12 opponents. Phillip scored in each of those games.

Hoping to rekindle their winning ways, the Buffaloes hosted the Arizona Wildcats on October 7. Phillip ran in a touchdown from 5 yards out in the first quarter and from a yard out in the second, helping his team keep pace with Arizona. At halftime, the Wildcats led, 21–14.

The third quarter was a back-and-forth affair. Arizona scored 2 touchdowns, while the Buffaloes continued to feed Phillip the football. His tough running helped to set up another Buffaloes' score.

Trailing 35–21 in the fourth quarter, CU mounted a ferocious comeback. They scored 3 touchdowns, including an 11-yard run by Phillip. But Arizona's 10 fourth-quarter points were enough to thwart the Buffaloes' rally, 45–42.

Phillip finished the day with an amazing 41 rushing attempts for 281 yards and 3 touchdowns. He chipped in another 3 receptions for 39 yards in the loss.

In desperate need of a victory to save their season, the Buffaloes again turned to Phillip. Against Oregon State, he ran the football 28 times for 185 yards and 2 touchdowns, including a 74-yard score. It was just enough to lift Colorado to a win, 36–33.

A disappointing loss to Washington State dropped Colorado's record to 4–4. The team rebounded against California with a stellar performance. Phillip was again the workhorse, carrying the ball 33 times and rushing for 166 yards. The Buffaloes never trailed on their way to a 44–28 victory.

Phillip didn't know it at the time, but that would prove to be his final win as a Buffalo. His team finished the season with 3 losses—and an overall record of 5–7.

Phillip's final home game was against the University of Southern California on November 11. The seniors were honored on the field before the contest. Phillip was joined by his mom and dad, and he invited someone else to be there with him: Michelle Brannigan, the learning specialist who had helped Phillip overcome his learning disability and gain success in the classroom.

On the day, Phillip rushed for 68 yards and scored a touchdown in CU's loss, 38–24. Afterward, Phillip was presented with the Buffalo Heart Award, a special honor from the team's passionate fans.

Phillip dives in for a touchdown against Oregon State.

In his final college game, Phillip rushed for 72 yards and a touchdown on the road against Utah, but the Buffaloes fell, 34–13.

On the year, Phillip rushed for 1,474 yards, the fifth most in the Pac-12 and the eleventh most in the entire National Collegiate Athletic Association (NCAA). It was also the fifth highest rushing total in CU history. His 301 rushing attempts tied for the most in the country and was a Buffaloes record. He scored 14 rushing touchdowns and 1 receiving touchdown to go along with his 23 receptions for 257 yards. His 144.3 all-purpose yards per game was the second best in the Pac-12 and earned him a spot on the All-Pac-12 second team at the all-purpose position.

Phillip was 1 of 11 semifinalists for the Doak Walker Award, given to the country's best college running back. He was named Colorado's Offensive Player of the Year by the Colorado Chapter of the National Football Foundation and College Hall of Fame. He was also given CU's Zack Jordan Award for the team's most valuable player and was again selected as the team's Best Interview.

EXTRA POINT

Phillip received an Eddie Crowder Award in the spring, for his leadership.

EXTRA POINT

During his college career, Phillip set or tied 26 school records on his way to becoming one of the best players in CU history. His impressive career statistics included the following:

- First in all-purpose yards: 5,760
- First in yards from scrimmage: 4,683
- First in receptions by a running back: 110
- First in receiving yards by a running back: 976
- Second in rushing yards: 3,707
- Fourth in total points scored: 234
- Sixth in kickoff return yards: 1,077

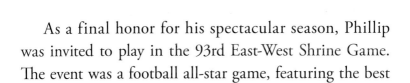

As a final honor for his spectacular season, Phillip was invited to play in the 93rd East-West Shrine Game. The event was a football all-star game, featuring the best college seniors from across the country.

Phillip donned the blue jersey of the West team for the charity exhibition game held on Saturday, January 20, 2018. It was a defensive struggle from beginning to end, but Phillip managed to shine. He led all rushers with 12 carries for 51 yards, and his team pulled off a come-from-behind victory to defeat the East All-Stars, 14–10.

12

Phillip's efforts in the classroom paid off, just as they had on the football field. He graduated from college in December of 2017. While most students finished college with a single degree, Phillip earned 2: one in communications and another in sociology.

After graduation, he set his sights on a new dream: the National Football League (NFL). Phillip had been one of the top running backs in all of college, and he believed that he was talented enough to play at the next level. He just needed to convince an NFL team to draft him. The 2018 NFL Scouting Combine was the place to do it.

The scouting combine would be held in Indianapolis, Indiana, from February 27 to March 5. Most of the top college players would be invited to this special event, where scouts from every NFL team studied the players as they performed various tests and challenges. This helped the scouts decide who would be good fits for their teams and which players they wanted the most.

Phillip needed to be in the best shape of his life to stand out among such spectacular athletes. He began working privately with Loren Landow, a trainer who specialized in preparing football players for the NFL. Six days a week,

Phillip spent his mornings at the South Suburban Sports Dome in Centennial, Colorado, sprinting and running drills to make himself faster. In the afternoons, he moved over to Landow Performance to lift weights and improve his overall strength.

His long days of extreme effort soon paid off. Phillip exercised his way into top physical condition. He was ready to dazzle the scouts at the combine—except for one very big and very surprising problem: Phillip didn't get invited to the combine!

Despite being one of the best running backs in CU history, despite being a top-15 rusher in the NCAA, despite shining in the East-West Shrine Game, Phillip was not among the 32 running backs chosen to attend. The news was devastating for a player who already felt uncertain that any team would pick him.

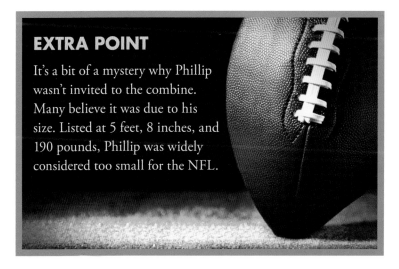

EXTRA POINT

It's a bit of a mystery why Phillip wasn't invited to the combine. Many believe it was due to his size. Listed at 5 feet, 8 inches, and 190 pounds, Phillip was widely considered too small for the NFL.

Phillip's disappointment turned to anger. He knew that he was good enough to attend the combine, and he knew that he was better than many of the players who had been invited. He let that anger drive him to work even harder. Fortunately, he still had one chance to get himself noticed by NFL scouts: CU's pro day.

Each university held a pro day in which scouts were allowed to come and watch the players from that university participate in combine-like drills. These opportunities allowed NFL teams to take a second look at players who attended the combine and a first look at players who didn't.

Colorado's pro day was held on Wednesday, March 7. Representatives from 29 teams attended to see Phillip and 15 other prospects perform. Phillip took full advantage of the pro day. He exceeded expectations at every turn. The event was highlighted by his 40-yard dash—a race that scouts used to determine whether a player was fast enough for the league. Phillip ran his 40-yard dash in an amazing 4.39 seconds, a time that would have placed second among running backs at the scouting combine!

Suddenly, there was talk that Phillip might have the makings of a good backup running back or wide receiver or even as a starting kickoff and punt returner.

The 2018 NFL draft took place from April 26 to 28. For 7 rounds, each team had an opportunity to choose a former college player for their team. Some teams also received bonus picks. All together, 256 players would be selected during the draft.

Phillip's 40-yard-dash time made him one of the draft's fastest backs.

It was a grueling weekend for Phillip and his family, spent waiting and hoping. Few expected that Phillip would get picked in the first 3 or 4 rounds, but many believed that his name would be called in a later round. There was even buzz that Phillip might be selected by his favorite team: the Denver Broncos.

Phillip stayed home for the draft and watched it on television. His family did their best to keep him occupied and distracted. They played games together, like cards and dominos. They left the house to get away from the news for a while. Yet Phillip's frustration grew with every pick. He couldn't understand why no one wanted him.

In the third round, Denver chose running back Royce Freeman. Would they take another running back later in the draft? The fourth round went by. The fifth and sixth rounds passed. Phillip's name had yet to be called. He put his hopes on the final round—and Denver's final pick.

The Broncos did select another running back . . .

David Williams from Arkansas.

Phillip's emotions ran wild. He jumped from hurt to shocked to angry to betrayed.

The rest of the draft flew by in a blur. All told, 20 running backs were selected—but not Phillip. Not one team believed in him enough to use a precious draft pick on him. Despite his record-breaking college career, Phillip had gone undrafted.

13

Because no team had drafted Phillip, he instantly became a free agent. He could play for the team of his choice . . . if any wanted him. Phillip wasn't sure that any of them did—but he didn't wonder for long.

As soon as the draft ended, his telephone started to ring. He was flooded with calls; it seemed that every team wanted him now, including Denver. But Phillip wasn't given much time to choose where to play. Teams were offering him just 15 minutes to decide his future.

Phillip still felt furious with the Broncos for not using 1 of their 10 draft picks on him. He was so upset that he no longer wanted to play for the team he had cheered since his youth. He decided to accept an offer from the Baltimore Ravens.

But before Phillip committed to them, his mom spoke up. She told her son that he should stay in Denver, that it was the right place for him to be.

Phillip had learned over the years that, when his mom offered advice, it was best to take it. His heart immediately softened to the idea, and it began to make sense. Denver's leading rusher from a year ago, C.J. Anderson, was no longer with the team. That meant the running back job

would be wide open, so Denver might be Phillip's best chance to win a roster spot. Plus, whether he earned a spot or not, he'd be close to home and would have his family nearby for support.

A few minutes later, Phillip spoke on the phone to the Broncos' representatives. He told them he was coming. He told them he was going to be their starting running back. And then he hung up on them.

Phillip signed with the Broncos for a $15,000 bonus. The amount was a nice start, but it wouldn't be enough to live on if he didn't make the team. So instead of getting his own place, he decided to stay at home with his parents. He turned the family basement into his new apartment.

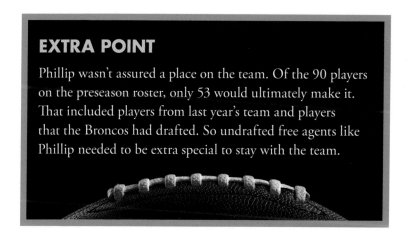

EXTRA POINT

Phillip wasn't assured a place on the team. Of the 90 players on the preseason roster, only 53 would ultimately make it. That included players from last year's team and players that the Broncos had drafted. So undrafted free agents like Phillip needed to be extra special to stay with the team.

From May 11 to 13, Phillip attended Denver's rookie minicamp. It provided an opportunity for the team's 10 draft picks and 8 rookie free agents to gain valuable information about the team and about playing in the NFL. These new players also had a chance to practice with their coaches.

Less than 2 weeks later, Phillip attended the Broncos' Organized Team Activities (OTAs), which began on May 22. OTAs included the team's veteran players, as well as the rookies.

Phillip impressed everyone with his work ethic, positive attitude, and ability to make plays. On the first day, he caught a deep pass from reserve quarterback Chad Kelly. Phillip also spent time returning punts, which suggested that he might become a key special teams player.

The buzz around Phillip continued into the summer and carried all the way to the start of training camp on July 28. On that first day, as the team began practicing for the 2018 season, Phillip stood out. He even caught the attention of defensive stars Brandon Marshall and Von Miller. Both players praised Phillip and imagined him playing a role on the team.

As the first week of training camp continued, Phillip gained a reputation for his excellent blocking skills and was also seen as a possible option to play wide receiver. On Day 7, though, Phillip dropped a couple of punts. The mistakes hurt his stock and reduced his chances of becoming the team's punt returner.

A few days later, on August 7, the Broncos unveiled their first depth chart, which showed where each player ranked at his position. For Phillip, there was both good news and bad news. The good news: He was listed as the team's starting kickoff returner. As for the bad news, he was at the very bottom of the running-back list. Five players were ahead of him.

If he couldn't find a way to move up the depth chart, he didn't know if the team would choose to keep him.

Phillip had 4 preseason games (practice games that didn't count as wins or losses) to impress his coaches and to prove that he belonged near the top of that list. If he didn't do that, he might find himself back at home, looking for a new job.

14

PRESEASON

Phillip's first opportunity to play in front of a stadium of Broncos fans came on August 11, in a preseason matchup against the Minnesota Vikings. The practice game helped veteran players get ready for the season ahead, and it provided a chance for young players like Phillip to show coaches what they could do in game situations.

EXTRA POINT

During the preseason, Phillip wore jersey number 2.

Phillip played just a handful of downs in the first half against the Vikings. He carried the ball once for 2 yards and caught a pass for 5 yards. But in the second half, he made a lasting impression.

Competing against third- and fourth-string players, Phillip showed himself to be one of the best talents on the field. His brightest moment came with 10 minutes left in the game. On 3rd down and 11 from the Vikings' 19-yard line, Phillip ran a quick pass route toward the middle of the field. He beat the Vikings defender and worked his way open. Reserve quarterback Chad Kelly spotted him and zipped the football to him. Phillip snagged the pass and sprinted the rest of the way to the end zone.

The touchdown play put Denver on top, 28–27, and revealed Phillip as a speedy offensive weapon. While the Broncos eventually fell, 42–28, Phillip opened plenty of eyes. He finished with 2 rushes for 7 yards and, more impressively, 3 receptions for 40 yards.

In Denver's second preseason contest, Phillip again saw little first-half action. But he was featured heavily in the third quarter. He ended up leading the team in rushing with 32 yards on 6 carries. The Broncos fell to the Chicago Bears, 24–23, but the starters and other key players performed well enough to win.

By the third preseason game, Phillip had earned playing time with the starting offense. He caught an 18-yard pass from quarterback Case Keenum on Denver's first drive, which helped to set up a field goal. Phillip played primarily with the first- and second-stringers and didn't see much action after the third quarter. He also remained Denver's top choice for kickoff returner. This suggested that the Broncos had already decided on Phillip; he would make the team.

Phillip finished with 31 yards rushing on 5 carries, and his team dominated the Washington Redskins from beginning to end. Denver won the game, 29–17.

The Broncos also won their final preseason contest against the Arizona Cardinals on August 30. Week 4 of the preseason was traditionally played without starters or other key personnel. So when Phillip was held out of the game, his spot on the final roster was assured. He might not get to play much during the regular season, but Phillip was a Denver Bronco.

When the time came to choose a new jersey number, Phillip knew what he wanted: number 30 to honor Terrell Davis. The beloved running back had played for the Broncos from 1995 to 2002, and he was a key player in Denver's championship runs in 1997 and 1998. In fact, he was the most valuable player of the team's first Super Bowl win, rushing for 157 yards and scoring 3 touchdowns.

Phillip didn't feel right just taking Davis's number. He had too much respect for the former player. So Phillip called him. He told Davis that, as a child, he used to find inspiration from a biography about him. Phillip then asked for permission to wear the number.

After talking with Phillip for a few minutes, Davis gladly gave Phillip his blessing.

15

🐎🐎🐎 PROMISING START 🐎🐎🐎

Phillip had made it onto the Broncos' final 53-man roster, and that was cause for celebration. He was in the NFL: a dream come true. But he was a third-string running back behind fellow rookie Royce Freeman and veteran Devontae Booker. The team hoped for greatness from Freeman, whom they had selected in the third round of the 2018 draft. Booker was a proven player with 2 years—and more than 250 rushing attempts—of experience. That didn't leave much room for Phillip to play or to make an impact in the games.

He would need to do his best with whatever chances he got, and the first of those came on September 9, when the Seattle Seahawks visited Broncos Stadium at Mile High. Phillip didn't expect to see any playing time, except for a handful of kickoffs and punts.

Not surprisingly, Denver started Freeman in the backfield. But the Broncos regularly shuffled their running backs in and out of the game. Freeman got his turn, and Booker did as well. Then, on the fifth play of the opening drive, with the ball at Denver's 35-yard line, Phillip was sent onto the field. Quarterback Case Keenum took the snap from center and handed it to his new running back.

Phillip dashed through the middle of the line, cut to his left, and scrapped his way forward for a 4-yard gain. The offense quieted after that.

Midway through the first quarter, Keenum threw an interception that set up a Seattle touchdown, giving the Seahawks a 7–0 lead. But the Broncos charged right back. On their next possession, a mix of Keenum passes and Freeman runs drove the offense to Seattle's 29-yard line. Phillip took the field for a second-down play. When the ball was snapped, he flared out to the left sideline and caught Keenum's short pass. But he didn't stop there. He turned upfield and accelerated.

His speed must have surprised the defense. Before the Seahawks could fully react, the rookie runner sprinted down the sideline and zoomed into the end zone. The home crowd roared, and Phillip celebrated his first NFL reception, his first NFL touchdown, and the first score of the Broncos' season. After a successful extra-point kick, the game was tied, 7–7.

EXTRA POINT

Phillip's parents attended the game and saw their son's touchdown.

At the beginning of the second quarter, Seattle reclaimed the lead with a field goal. Once again, the

Broncos responded. Their next drive went 75 yards in 6 plays, including runs of 9 and 6 yards by Phillip. A 43-yard touchdown catch and run by wide receiver Emmanuel Sanders capped the drive and gave Denver its first lead, 14–10.

The Broncos added a field goal and went into halftime ahead by 7 points. While all 3 Denver runners had carried the ball multiple times, Phillip was the standout. *NFL on FOX* television announcers Dick Stockton and Mark Schlereth referred to him as "special" and "a wonder."

The team's momentum, however, didn't carry into the third quarter. The offense stalled, and the defense gave up the tying touchdown, 17–17. But late in the third, while the offense couldn't get anything going, the defense made something happen. Safety Justin Simmons intercepted a pass in Seattle territory. It set up a 53-yard field goal by Brandon McManus that again put Denver in front.

They did not hold the lead for long. The Seahawks began the fourth quarter with a 51-yard touchdown bomb from quarterback Russell Wilson to speedy receiver Tyler Lockett. Seattle led, 24–20.

The Broncos needed a touchdown, so the offense went back to work. Phillip sparked the comeback drive with a run of 14 yards and then another for 5 yards. Keenum took over from there, completing 5 straight passes for 61 yards, including a 4-yard touchdown to wide receiver Demaryius Thomas. The play gave Denver a 27–24 lead, a score that would hold up until time ran out on the Seahawks.

Phillip began as Denver's third back, but by the end of the game, he was the featured runner. He finished tied with Freeman as the team's leading rusher, gaining 71 yards on 15 carries. Phillip also added 2 receptions for 31 yards.

It was an impressive debut for the undrafted rookie. But was it enough to move him up from the third spot on the depth chart?

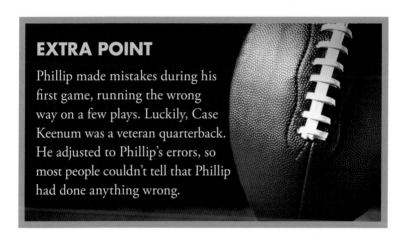

EXTRA POINT

Phillip made mistakes during his first game, running the wrong way on a few plays. Luckily, Case Keenum was a veteran quarterback. He adjusted to Phillip's errors, so most people couldn't tell that Phillip had done anything wrong.

16

The second week of the season brought the rival Oakland Raiders to the Mile High City. The 92-degree temperature made it the hottest Denver game in 27 years. Royce Freeman was again named the starting running back, but Phillip and Devontae Booker would surely see their share of action.

As hot as the day was, the Broncos offense started ice cold. The only highlight of the first half came early in the second quarter. Phillip took a handoff from Case Keenum, dashed through the middle of the line, and wove through the defense to the right sideline. He wasn't stopped until 53 yards later, when he was bumped out of bounds at the 22-yard line. The drive ended 3 plays later when Keenum threw an interception.

The Raiders offense fared better, tallying 2 field goals and a touchdown before halftime. After a blocked extra point, Oakland led 12–0.

The Broncos began the third quarter with a new plan: run the football. On their opening drive, Denver called 6 straight running plays. Phillip and Freeman carried the Broncos all the way to Oakland's 15-yard line. Then, after

Keenum's arm hurled the team down to the 1-yard line, Freeman finished the drive with a touchdown plunge up the middle.

Denver finally gained some momentum, but it didn't last long. Raiders quarterback Derek Carr led a 75-yard touchdown drive that took just 6 plays. The visiting team extended its lead to 19–7.

The Broncos added a field goal, and the defense kept Oakland from scoring. Denver took over possession of the football early in the fourth quarter and strung together their longest drive of the day: 14 plays—and more than 7 minutes. Along the way, Phillip carried the ball 5 times for 22 yards, getting his team all the way to the 1-yard line. Keenum dove into the end zone on a gutsy fourth-down play, cutting the deficit to 19–17.

The Denver defense again held strong, forcing Oakland to punt. With just 1:58 left in the game, the Broncos needed a score to win. As time ticked away, Keenum coolly completed 4 passes for 65 yards, guiding his team to the Raiders' 18-yard line.

With just 6 seconds on the clock, Brandon McManus kicked the Broncos to a 20–19 victory!

It was an impressive comeback win—and another impressive performance by Phillip. The rookie runner tallied a team-high 107 yards rushing on 14 carries, along with 1 catch for 4 yards. His performance made him the first undrafted player ever to gain more than 100 total yards from scrimmage in his first 2 NFL games.

Two days later, Phillip visited West High School in Denver. He spoke with the football team, hoping to inspire them the way Willis McGahee inspired him back in 2012.

The following Sunday, the Broncos tried to continue their winning ways. They traveled to Baltimore to battle the Ravens in their first road game of the season. While the weather had been scorching the week before, this game saw rainy conditions that made the field slippery and wet.

The foul weather didn't slow either team in the first quarter. Denver scored 2 quick touchdowns to take a 14–7 lead 8 minutes into the game. Unfortunately, Denver's highlights ended there.

In the second quarter, the Ravens rallied ahead, 17–14. Then, in the final minutes of the half, Case Keenum fumbled, creating a wild skirmish to get the loose ball.

Phillip dove into the scramble, and he saw a chance to grab the football. At the same moment, a Ravens defender went for it too. Phillip tried to punch the ball away, but an official thought he was punching the other player.

The referee called a penalty on Phillip . . . and ejected him from the game!

After losing their leading rusher—the third leading rusher in the NFL—Denver's offense never got on track again. The team fell, 27–14.

Afterward, Phillip said that he let his team down, and he promised that it would never happen again. He looked forward to getting back on the field and helping his team in Week 4, when the Broncos would return home to face the high-powered Kansas City Chiefs.

Panoramic view of Denver Broncos Stadium at Mile High

17

LIGHTNING

By October 1, the Kansas City Chiefs were already considered one of the best teams in football. They were 3–0 and had scored an average of 39 points per game. Their quarterback, first-year starter Patrick Mahomes, had thrown 13 touchdown passes—an NFL record for the most ever in the first 3 weeks of a season. So when they came to Broncos Stadium at Mile High for a nationally televised matchup on Monday Night Football, most of the country expected them to win. The Broncos, however, had other plans.

Denver got on the board early, thanks in part to a 17-yard burst by Phillip. It led to a field goal. Kansas City answered with a field goal of their own. The Chiefs added a touchdown midway through the second quarter, giving them a 10–3 lead. But the Broncos closed out the half with 10 straight points.

Denver's defense looked impressive, holding the record-setting offense to just 2 scores. On the other side of the ball, the Broncos' rookie tandem of runners were stealing the show. Phillip and Royce Freeman complemented each other perfectly. They were like thunder and lightning. Freeman was the tough, rumbling, powerful back, the "thunder." Phillip was the small, agile, quick back, the "lightning." Together, they had kept the offense moving—and kept the Chiefs' offense off the field—combining for 88 yards on 10 attempts.

The trend continued in the third quarter. After Kansas City tied the game, 13–13, the Broncos' backs took over, leading their team on a 9-play, 80-yard drive. Phillip carried most of the load, running 5 times for 26 yards, including a 1-yard touchdown plunge.

The Broncos added a field goal in the early minutes of the fourth quarter to take a commanding 23–13 lead. But Kansas City was considered a Super Bowl contender for good reason. Mahomes rallied his team for 2 late touchdowns, giving the visitors a 27–23 victory in one of the most entertaining games of the season.

Phillip and Freeman finished the day with a combined 20 carries for 136 yards and 2 rushing touchdowns. Phillip also added 10 yards receiving and a 32-yard kickoff return.

The loss dropped Denver's record to 2–2. They hoped to regain their winning ways with a trip northeast to face the New York Jets.

That day belonged to New York's tandem of runners. Isaiah Crowell rushed for 219 yards—the most ever by a Jet. Bilal Powell chipped in another 99 yards en route to a 34–16 win for New York. Phillip led the Broncos with 61 yards rushing in the loss.

The slide continued when the undefeated Los Angeles Rams came to town. All-star running back Todd Gurley rushed for 208 yards, and the Rams jumped ahead, 20–3. The Broncos put together a second-half rally but fell short, 23–20. Phillip carried the ball just 4 times for 18 yards in the loss; he added 6 receptions for 48 yards receiving.

With a record of 2–4, Denver was in danger of letting their playoff hopes slip away before the season was half over. They were in desperate need of a victory, and their next game was just 4 days away: a nationally televised matchup on Thursday, October 18, against the Arizona Cardinals.

Phillip also became known among Denver fans for his famous hairdo.

18

The Broncos traveled to Glendale, Arizona, knowing that the contest against the 1–5 Cardinals was a must-win game. Pro Bowl linebacker Von Miller predicted a victory, and his defense accepted the challenge to prove him right.

The team scored 3 first-quarter touchdowns, including 2 interceptions returned for touchdowns. The Broncos' domination continued throughout the rest of the game, and the final result was never in doubt. Phillip's team steamrolled the Cardinals, 45–10, and the rookie back contributed 90 yards on 14 rushes, including a 28-yard touchdown run in the third quarter.

The Broncos hoped their newfound momentum would carry over to Week 8, a rematch against the division-leading Kansas City Chiefs. The Chiefs' record stood at 6–1, and the team was playing at home. Denver was without its starting running back, Royce Freeman, due to an ankle injury. So Phillip was promoted to starter, and he would be a vital part of the Broncos' game plan.

Midway through the first quarter, Denver put together an 8-play, 81-yard drive. Phillip capped the drive with a 1-yard touchdown run, giving his team a 7–0 lead.

The next quarter and a half belonged to Kansas City. They reeled off 16 straight points, including a touchdown with just 54 seconds left in the half. It appeared that the Chiefs would go into halftime with a commanding 9-point lead. But Case Keenum orchestrated a masterful 5-play, 75-yard drive in just 49 seconds. He threw a 24-yard touchdown pass to receiver Tim Patrick with just 5 seconds on the clock, cutting Kansas City's lead to 16–14.

The third quarter belonged to the Chiefs. They scored touchdowns on their first 2 possessions, catapulting them to a 30–14 advantage. Meanwhile, the Broncos gave up a sack and committed 3 costly penalties that negated runs by Phillip of 23 and 27 yards, as well as a 10-yard reception.

Nevertheless, the Broncos bounced back. Keenum connected with tight end Jeff Heuerman on a 4-yard touchdown pass as the fourth quarter began. But the Broncos turned the ball over on their next 2 possessions.

They added a field goal with less than 2 minutes to go, giving themselves a chance at 30–23. But their attempt at an onside kick failed, and the Chiefs were all but able to run out the clock.

Phillip proved his worth as a starter, rushing for 95 yards and a touchdown, despite 2 of his biggest plays being called back on penalties. The loss dropped his team to 3–5 on the season.

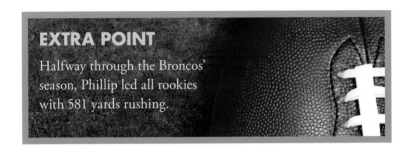

Two days later, the team made a difficult decision. They traded popular wide receiver Demaryius Thomas to the Houston Texans for a fourth-round draft pick. Thomas had been with the Broncos for more than 8 years, but the team wanted more playing time for his backup, rookie Courtland Sutton. So they sent Thomas to a team that needed him more.

In a twist of fate, Thomas didn't go far for his next game. His new team, the Texans, came to town. He would play in Denver once more—this time as a visitor.

The tough Texans defense did a good job of containing Phillip for most of the game. He finished with 17 carries for 60 yards in a low-scoring contest.

The Broncos kept pace with Houston, and they put themselves in position to win. But the home team missed a 51-yard field goal on the final play of the game.

They lost a heartbreaker, 19–17, giving Houston its sixth straight victory.

19

FIELD GOAL FINISH

Denver's schedule didn't get easier. On November 18, after a bye week, the team traveled to Los Angeles to face the Chargers, who were riding a 6-game winning streak of their own.

The home team managed 2 early field goals, and the Chargers defense dominated the first quarter, holding the Broncos to just 34 total yards. That trend continued into the second quarter. After 4 plays, the Broncos offense was forced into another punting situation.

The team needed a spark, and Denver's coaching staff knew just how to get it. The ball was snapped to punter Colby Wadman on fourth down, but he didn't punt. Instead, he rolled to his left and tossed a short pass to fullback Andy Janovich, who barreled ahead 12 yards to the Chargers' 41-yard line. The trick play was more than enough to give Denver a first down.

On the very next play, Case Keenum handed off to Phillip. The Broncos' leading rusher hesitated for a moment, waiting for a hole to open. Then he burst through the middle of the offensive line, cut to his left, and dashed all the way to the end zone for a touchdown. The 41-yard score put Denver ahead, 7–6.

Los Angeles reclaimed the lead before halftime, when quarterback Philip Rivers connected with receiver Keenan Allen. They extended that lead with a 9-play, 75-yard drive to open the third quarter. This time, Rivers hit tight end Antonio Gates for a 6-yard score.

Down 19–7 and on the road against one of the league's top teams, it looked as if the Broncos were about to get blown out. To make matters the worse, the offense could not get going. Outside of Phillip's scoring play, Denver had only managed 105 total yards.

It would take another big play to get them back in the game—and the Broncos defense responded. The Chargers were driving toward another score late in the third quarter when Rivers attempted a screen pass to his right. All-Pro linebacker Von Miller stepped into the ball's path, reached up, and intercepted the football. He ran for 42 yards, all the way to the Chargers' 18-yard line before he was tackled from behind.

The turnover set up the Broncos for a quick touchdown 3 plays later. Royce Freeman rushed the ball into the end zone from 3 yards out. Los Angeles's lead was cut to 19–14.

On their next possession, Denver kept rolling. Keenum marched his offense 73 yards. Phillip finished the drive early in the fourth quarter, running around the left side of the offensive line for a 2-yard touchdown. The Broncos edged ahead, 20–19.

Los Angeles came back with a field goal on their next possession, putting them ahead by 2. That's where the

score remained until Denver received the ball on their 8-yard line with just 1:51 to play.

With a last chance to steal a win, Keenum completed 5 straight passes, including a 38-yard catch-and-run by Emmanuel Sanders and a 30-yard bomb to Courtland Sutton. That put Denver in position for a field goal attempt from the 16-yard line.

With just 3 seconds on the clock, kicker Brandon McManus drilled his kick through the goal posts, lifting Denver to one of their most thrilling victories of the season—an upset over their division rival, 23–22.

Phillip led the way with 79 yards rushing, 27 yards receiving, and 2 touchdowns.

20

BIG WINS

The dramatic victory against the Chargers improved Denver's record to 4–6, and it kept their playoff hopes alive. But in order to qualify for the postseason, the Broncos needed to win at least 5 of their final 6 games.

Unfortunately, Denver's incredibly difficult stretch of opponents continued. For the third game in a row, they would play a team that had won 5 straight. This time, the 7–2–1 Pittsburgh Steelers were visiting.

Pittsburgh moved the ball well to start the game, but the Broncos defenders kept them off the scoreboard with big plays. Safety Justin Simmons blocked a field goal, and safety Will Parks forced a fumble at the goal line; the play that would have been a touchdown became a turnover.

The Broncos pulled ahead by 10 points, but the visitors finished their final 2 drives of the half with scores. The teams went into the locker room at halftime, tied at 10–10.

Pittsburgh captured momentum in the third quarter when quarterback Ben Roethlisberger threw a 97-yard touchdown pass to wide receiver JuJu Smith-Schuster. A few minutes later, the Steelers looked ready to add to that lead, but cornerback Chris Harris, Jr., intercepted a pass.

Two plays after that, Case Keenum tied the game with a 5-yard touchdown pass to Emmanuel Sanders.

The Steelers' mistakes continued. They again drove the football into scoring range but fumbled away their opportunity at the end of the third quarter.

Phillip and the Broncos took advantage. On their first possession of the fourth quarter, Phillip reeled off runs of 9 and 18 yards, helping his team move all the way to Pittsburgh's 2-yard line. There, Phillip took a handoff from Keenum and bulldozed his way forward, into the end zone. The play gave Denver a 24–17 lead.

As the final minutes ticked away, the Steelers' had just one more chance. Roethlisberger guided his team 54 yards on 9 plays, and the Steelers found themselves at Denver's 2-yard line.

The Broncos were in danger of letting Pittsburgh tie the score. Roethlisberger caught the snap from center, faked a handoff, and then he tossed the ball into the middle of the end zone. He didn't see defensive lineman Shelby Harris pretend to rush and then drop back into coverage. Roethlisberger threw an interception right to him—and Denver's victory was secured.

Phillip was a difference-maker on that day. He carried the football 14 times and racked up 110 yards on the ground, including the game-winning touchdown.

A week later, Phillip played his best game of the year. He rushed 19 times for 157 yards and 2 touchdowns, including his longest run: 65 yards on a sweep down the left sideline. The Broncos defeated the Bengals, 24–10, for their third straight victory.

EXTRA POINT

Phillip's performance against the Bengals earned him 3 awards: FexEx Ground Player of the Week, Pepsi Rookie of the Week, and AFC Offensive Player of the Week.

With a record of 6–6, Denver was back in the middle of the playoff race. The schedule finally favored them too. Three of their last 4 games were against teams with losing records. All the Broncos had to do was take care of business and keep winning.

21

🐎🐎🐎🐎 BUSTED HOPES 🐎🐎🐎🐎

Denver was peaking at the right time. They were playing their best football when it mattered the most: at the end of the season. Many experts believed that the team would win their next 3 games, and their chances of making the playoffs would come down to the final game of the season.

But the Broncos' hopes took a major hit during practice on Wednesday, December 5. Star wide receiver Emmanuel Sanders tore the Achilles tendon in his left leg. The severe injury ended his season, making rookie Courtland Sutton the team's number-one receiver.

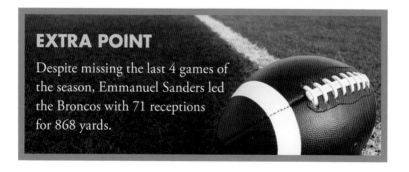

EXTRA POINT

Despite missing the last 4 games of the season, Emmanuel Sanders led the Broncos with 71 receptions for 868 yards.

Four days later, Denver took the field in San Francisco against the 49ers. The 2–10 team was not expected to win, but they played one of their best games. Without Sanders on the field, the 49ers could focus on stopping Phillip and the other Broncos runners.

Their game plan worked. Denver managed just 2 touchdowns, and Phillip was held to 30 yards rushing. The Broncos lost, 20–14.

Their playoff hopes were hanging by a thread; the team would be eliminated with one more loss. So when the 5–7–1 Cleveland Browns came to Broncos Stadium at Mile High for a Saturday night showdown, Denver turned to its best offensive weapon: Phillip Lindsay.

The Broncos tried to get Phillip the ball on 5 of their first 6 plays. But with the Browns keying on him, those plays netted -4 yards and led to 2 quick punts. Both defenses dominated, and the teams played to a 10–10 tie at halftime.

The Broncos pulled ahead in the third quarter with a field goal, but the Browns answered with a touchdown early in the fourth. Denver added another field goal, and they had a chance to steal a win in the game's final minute. But the offense stalled at the 50-yard line. The home team fell to Cleveland, 17–16, officially eliminating them from the playoffs.

Phillip was held to 24 yards rushing on 14 attempts, along with 4 catches for 20 yards receiving.

The Broncos continued to struggle the following week, on the road against the Oakland Raiders—on Christmas

Eve. Denver fell behind 17–0, and the offense couldn't get going until midway through the third quarter. The team finally strung together an 8-play, 82-yard drive that ended with a 7-yard touchdown pass from Keenum to receiver DaeSean Hamilton. But it was a costly drive.

One play before the score, Phillip took a handoff, hesitated at the line, and then sliced through an opening. Seven yards later, Phillip reached out his right arm as he was hit by 2 Raiders safeties. The impact severely injured his wrist.

With their leading rusher and their leading receiver out, Denver fell to Oakland, 27–14.

Phillip and his team traveled home overnight, and Phillip reached his parents' home at around 4 a.m. on Christmas morning. A few hours later, his father took him to get an MRI on his wrist.

The news wasn't good. His wrist would require surgery; his season was over.

It was a disappointing outcome, to say the least, but Phillip wouldn't let that ruin the holiday. His entire family, including all 4 of his siblings, came together that evening. They enjoyed a traditional dinner, and Phillip surprised his parents with gifts. His mom received a microwave, refrigerator, and stove. His dad got a brand-new recliner to sit in.

A few days later, Phillip had surgery on his wrist. Doctors hoped that it would fully heal within 3 to 5 months.

The Broncos dropped their final game of the season, 24–9, to the Los Angeles Chargers. With four straight losses to end the 2018 season, they finished with a record of 6–10.

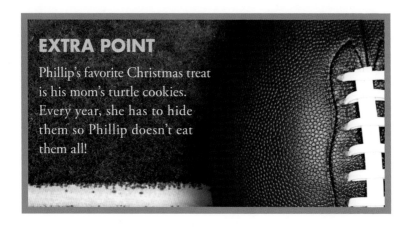

EXTRA POINT

Phillip's favorite Christmas treat is his mom's turtle cookies. Every year, she has to hide them so Phillip doesn't eat them all!

EPILOGUE

Although Phillip's season ended too soon, he made a name for himself on—and off—the field. He finished with 1,037 yards rushing and 9 rushing touchdowns. He added 241 yards receiving and a receiving touchdown. His total rushing yards ranked 9th highest—the 2nd best among rookies. His average of 5.4 yards per rushing attempt was 2nd best in the league. He was only the third undrafted running back ever to top 1,000 yards rushing in a season.

On December 18, 2018, Phillip was named to the 2019 Pro Bowl, an all-star game at the end of January that featured the best players in the league. Phillip became the first undrafted offensive rookie ever to make the Pro Bowl team. Unfortunately, his injury did not allow him to play, but Phillip attended as a special correspondent—to help the NFL cover the event on social media.

Phillip was 1 of 5 players nominated for the 2018 Pepsi NFL Rookie of the Year award. While the honor ultimately went to New York Giants running back Saquon Barkley, the nomination itself exemplified how far Phillip had come in just one season.

He received the VIZIO Top Value Performer award, given to the player who surpassed preseason expectations to help his team more than any other.

Phillip was also recognized by the Colorado Sports Hall of Fame as the 2018 Colorado Professional Athlete of the Year. He was honored on April 3, 2019, at the 55th Annual Colorado Sports Hall of Fame Induction & Awards Banquet.

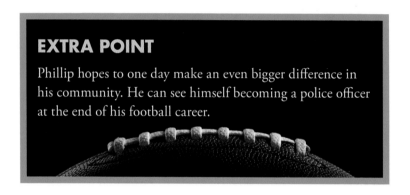

EXTRA POINT

Phillip hopes to one day make an even bigger difference in his community. He can see himself becoming a police officer at the end of his football career.

In 2018, Phillip surprised Broncos fans—and football fans everywhere. In just one NFL season, he went from an undrafted rookie who might not make the team to one of the most explosive offensive players in the league. But his story didn't end there. Phillip continued to work hard, to improve his skills, and to maintain a winning attitude. He believed that, in the seasons to come, he could help the Broncos improve and earn their way into the playoffs—maybe even bring another National Football League championship home to Colorado.

Amazing Sports Biographies

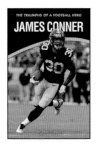

JAMES CONNER

A historic college career was derailed by a severe injury—and then a terrifying cancer diagnosis. Yet he rose to become one of the NFL's best running backs.

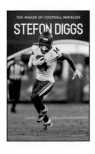

STEFON DIGGS

He overcame high school tragedy and a severe college injury and is perhaps best known for one of the greatest plays in NFL playoff history.

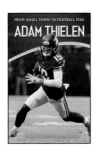

ADAM THIELEN

He couldn't find a college football team that wanted him, yet he worked his way from tryouts, to practice squad, to special teams, to all-star wide receiver.

Read all the incredible true stories of athletes who achieved their dreams through hard work, dedication, and perseverance. The Amazing Sports Biographies are available wherever books are sold.

SOURCES

"2016 Colorado Buffaloes Stats." Sports Reference (sports-reference.com). Accessed on April 23, 2019.

"About the National Letter of Intent." National Letter of Intent (nationalletter.org). Accessed on April 6, 2019.

Alvarez, Nick. "Colorado's Phillip Lindsay Relies on Family, Football, to Enact the Change He Wants to See." The Daily Orange (dailyorange.com). October 26, 2017.

AP. "Phillip Lindsay Has Gone from Undrafted to Unforgettable." Fox Sports (foxsports.com). September 17, 2018.

AP. "Tailback Dubbed Tasmanian Devil Leads Colorado's Revival." *USA Today* (usatoday.com). October 12, 2016.

Brady, James. "NFL Draft Results 2018: Full List of Selections for All 7 Rounds." SB Nation (sbnation.com). April 28, 2018.

Brinson, Will. "Emmanuel Sanders Injury Update: Torn Achilles Ends Receiver's Season and Possibly Broncos Career Too." CBS Sports (cbssports.com). December 5, 2018.

"Broncos OTA Day 1 Observations." Denver Broncos (denverbroncos.com). May 22, 2018.

Casey, Ryan. *The Denver Post* (denverpost.com).
- "Denver South Running Back Phillip Lindsay, CU Commit, Tears ACL." September 19, 2012.
- "High School Football Rankings: Columbine Takes over as 5A's No. 1." September 4, 2012.

Colorado Buffaloes (cubuffs.com)
- 2017 Football Schedule. Accessed on February 25, 2019.
- 2016 Football Schedule. Accessed on February 25, 2019.
- 2015 Football Schedule. Accessed on February 25, 2019.
- 2014 Football Schedule. Accessed on February 25, 2019.
- 2013 Football Schedule. Accessed on February 25, 2019.
- Arizona vs. Colorado. October 7, 2017.
- Northern Colorado vs. Colorado. September 16, 2017.
- Colorado State vs. Colorado. September 1, 2017.

- Colorado vs. Washington. December 2, 2016.
- Arizona State vs. Colorado. October 15, 2016.
- Colorado vs. USC. October 8, 2016.
- Colorado vs. Oregon. September 24, 2016.
- Colorado vs. Oregon State. October 24, 2015.
- Colorado vs. Colorado State. September 19, 2015.
- Colorado vs. Arizona. November 8, 2014.
- "Phillip Lindsay." Accessed on February 25, 2019.

"CU Recruit Took Long Road from Setback to Signing Day." Denver CBS(4) (denver.cbslocal.com). February 10, 2013.

"Dermatomyositis." Mayo Clinic (mayoclinic.org). Accessed on May 22, 2019.

East-West Shrine Game (shrinegame.com). Accessed on April 20, 2018.

ESPN (espn.com)
- Arizona State vs. Colorado. October 15, 2016.
- UMass vs. Colorado. September 12, 2015.

"Former Futures Football Player Phillip Lindsay Inspires Next Generation." Priority Sports (prioritysports.biz). June 4, 2018.

Frederickson, Kyle. *The Denver Post* (denverpost.com).
- "Colorado Buffaloes Running Back Phillip Lindsay's Dad Was a Colorado State Ram. August 31, 2017.
- "Broncos Report to Rookie Mini-Camp with Large Corps of Former College Team Captains." May 11, 2018.
- "An Oral History of Unlikely Broncos Running Back Phillip Lindsay. 'He's Not Scared of Anybody.' " September 15, 2018.

"Futures Football Kicks off 10th Season with the Broncos' Help." Denver Broncos (denverbroncos.com). March 5, 2018.

Heath, Jon. Broncos Wire (broncoswire.usatoday.com).
- "Broncos RB Phillip Lindsay Surpasses 1,000 Yards Rushing." December 24, 2018.
- "Phillip Lindsay Named Colorado Professional Athlete of the Year." January 10, 2019.

Howell, Brian. Daily Camera (dailycamera.com).
- "CU Football: Pride Drives Buffs' RB Phillip Lindsay." August 20, 2014.
- "CU's Phillip Lindsay: 'My Father Is Everything.' " June 20, 2015.

Howell, Brian. "Lindsay Brothers Ready for Emotional Game Between Buffs and Bears." BuffZone (buffzone.com). September 15, 2017.

Jensen, Chad. "Phillip Lindsay's Mom Changed His Opinion on Signing with Denver." Denver CBS(4) (denver.cbslocal.com). December 2, 2018.

Jhabvala, Nicki. "Denied an NFL Scouting Combine Invite, Former CU Buffs Star Phillip Lindsay Is out to Prove 'em Wrong." *The Denver Post* (denverpost.com). February 13, 2018.

Kazmierczak, Anthony. "Phillip Lindsay Had a Fantastic Pro Day." SB Nation: The Ralphie Report (ralphiereport.com). March 8, 2018.

Kelberman, Zack. "Highlights from Denver Broncos' Rookie Minicamp Practice." 247 Sports (247sports.com). May 13, 2018.

Kelberman, Zack. "Phillip Lindsay Felt 'Horrible' About Ejection: 'I Let My Team Down.' " Denver CBS(4) (denver.cbslocal.com). September 24, 2018.

Kirshner, Alex. SB Nation (sbnation.com).
- "How Rare It Is to Be a 5-star (or Even a 2-, 3-, or 4-star) College Football Recruit." January 30, 2019.
- "J.T. Barrett (and Everyone Else) Had a Hard Time Moving the Ball in the East-West Shrine Game." January 20, 2018.

Klis, Mike; "Phillip Lindsay on Offseason Snub: 'The Combine's Cute.' " 9 News (9news.com). September 16, 2018.

Klee, Paul. "Paul Klee: CU's Phillip Lindsay Is Doing It Again—This Time in Denver Broncos Training Camp." *The Gazette* (gazette.com). July 30, 2018.

Legwold, Jeff. "Phillip Lindsay Tossed from Broncos Game After Throwing Punch." ESPN (espn.com). September 23, 2018.

Light, Casey. "Phillip Lindsay's 2018 NFL Scouting Combine Snub Is Baffling." Mile High Sports (milehighsports.com). February 26, 2018.

Lynch, Tim. SB Nation: Mile High Report (milehighreport.com).
- "Denver Broncos Release First Depth Chart of 2018." August 7, 2018.
- "Key Takeaways from Denver Broncos OTA's." June 15, 2018.

MaxPreps (maxpreps.com). Accessed on March 5, 2019.
- Denver South 2012 Football Schedule
- Denver South 2011 Football Schedule
- Denver South 2010 Football Schedule
- Denver South 2009 Football Schedule
- Bear Creek vs. Denver South. November 3, 2011.
- Denver South vs. Golden. September 1, 2011.
- Denver South vs. Arapahoe. November 6, 2010.
- Lakewood vs. Denver South. October 8, 2010.
- Golden vs. Denver South. September 4, 2010.
- Denver South vs. Golden. September 3, 2009.
- Phillip Lindsay
- Phillip Lindsay's Football Stats
- Zachary Lindsay's Football Stats

Munsterteiger, Adam. "Lindsay Motivated by His Mother." Rivals: CU Sports Nation (colorado.rivals.com). April 10, 2014.

Nesbitt, Andy. "Broncos Rookie Phillip Lindsay Makes Pretty Cool NFL History by Being Named to Pro Bowl." *USA Today* (usatoday.com). December 19, 2018.

Newman, Kyle. "The Broncos' Futures Program Saved Football in Denver Public Schools. But an Even Bigger Impact of the Feeder Teams Might Still Be Seen." *The Denver Post* (denverpost.com). April 8, 2018.

"NFL Attendance - 2018." ESPN (espn.com). Accessed on May 22, 2019.

"NFL Game Center." NFL (nfl.com).
- Los Angeles Chargers vs. Denver. December 30, 2018.
- Denver vs. Oakland. December 24, 2018.
- Cleveland vs. Denver. December 15, 2018.
- Denver vs. San Francisco. December 9, 2018.
- Denver vs. Cincinnati. December 2, 2018.
- Pittsburgh vs. Denver. November 25, 2018.
- Denver vs. Los Angeles Chargers. November 18, 2018.
- Houston vs. Denver. November 4, 2018.
- Denver vs. Kansas City. October 28, 2018.
- Denver vs. Arizona. October 18, 2018.
- Los Angeles Rams vs. Denver. October 14, 2018.
- Denver vs. New York Jets. October 7, 2018.
- Kansas City vs. Denver. October 1, 2018.
- Denver vs. Baltimore. September 23, 2018.

- Oakland vs. Denver. September 16, 2018.
- Seattle vs. Denver. September 9, 2018.
- Denver vs. Arizona. August 30, 2018.
- Denver vs. Washington. August 24, 2018.
- Chicago vs. Denver. August 18, 2018.
- Minnesota vs. Denver. August 11, 2018.

NFL Game Pass (gamepass.nfl.com).
- Denver vs. Oakland. December 24, 2018.
- Cleveland vs. Denver. December 15, 2018.
- Denver vs. San Francisco. December 9, 2018.
- Denver vs. Cincinnati. December 2, 2018.
- Pittsburgh vs. Denver. November 25, 2018.
- Denver vs. Los Angeles Chargers. November 18, 2018.
- Houston vs. Denver. November 4, 2018.
- Denver vs. Kansas City. October 28, 2018.
- Denver vs. Arizona. October 18, 2018.
- Los Angeles Rams vs. Denver. October 14, 2018.
- Denver vs. New York Jets. October 7, 2018.
- Kansas City vs. Denver. October 1, 2018.
- Denver vs. Baltimore. September 23, 2018.
- Oakland vs. Denver. September 16, 2018.
- Seattle vs. Denver. September 9, 2018.
- Denver vs. Washington. August 24, 2018.
- Chicago vs. Denver. August 18, 2018.
- Minnesota vs. Denver. August 11, 2018.

"NFL History - Super Bowl MVPs." ESPN (espn.com). Accessed on April 24, 2019.

"NFL Players" (nfl.com).
- "Demaryius Thomas." Accessed on March 19, 2019.
- "Devontae Booker." Accessed on March 19, 2019.
- "Phillip Lindsay." Accessed on March 19, 2019.
- "Terrell Davis." Accessed on April 24, 2019.

O'Halloran, Ryan. *The Denver Post* (denverpost.com).
- "Phillip Lindsay at the Pro Bowl: Spectator This Year, Participant Next Year." January 27, 2019.
- "Broncos Briefs: Surgeon Details What Phillip Lindsay's Rehabilitation Will Entail." December 27, 2018.

"Pac-12 Football Standings - 2012." ESPN (espn.com). Accessed on March 20, 2019.

Patra, Kevin. "Texans Trade for Broncos WR Demaryius Thomas." NFL (nfl.com). October 30, 2018.

Payne, Scotty. SB Nation: Mile High Report (milehighreport.com).
- "Denver Broncos Training Camp: Day 7 News and Notes." August 4, 2018.
- "Denver Broncos Training Camp: Day 5 News and Notes." August 1, 2018.
- "Denver Broncos Training Camp: Day 4 News and Notes." July 31, 2018.
- "Denver Broncos Training Camp: Day 3 News and Notes." July 30, 2018.
- "Denver Broncos Training Camp: Day 1 News and Notes." July 28, 2018.

"Pepsi Rookie of the Year - 2018." NFL (nfl.com). Accessed on March 28, 2019.

"Phillip Lindsay." Rivals (n.rivals.com). Accessed on March 6, 2019.

"Phillip Lindsay Finally Wins Rookie of the Week, Also Garners Ground Player Award." Denver CBS(4) (denver.cbslocal.com). December 7, 2018.

Place, Jess. "Horse Tracks: Broncos Rookie Minicamp in the Books." SB Nation: Mile High Report (milehighreport.com). May 14, 2018.

Pro Football Reference (pro-football-reference.com).
- "2018 NFL Rushing." Accessed on April 2, 2019.
- "Phillip Lindsay." Accessed on April 20, 2019.
- "Quentin Griffin." Accessed on May 22, 2019.

Pompei, Dan. "How Phillip Lindsay Went from Undrafted to Pro Bowl—Without Ever Leaving Home." Bleacher Report (bleacherreport.com), December 27, 2018.

Rajendran, Kartik. "Oklahoma Sooners Football: A Tribute to Recent OU Graduate Quentin Griffin." SB Nation: Crimson and Cream Machine (crimsonandcreammachine.com). May 17, 2017.

Stephenson, Zora. "Phillip Lindsay's Sisters Share Their Common Bond." Fox 31 Denver (kdvr.com). December 14, 2018.

Swanson, Ben. "How Phillip Lindsay's Roots Guide His Devotion to the Denver Community." Denver Broncos (denverbroncos.com). September 18, 2018.

"TVP: Phillip Lindsay." VIZIO (tvp.vizio.com). Accessed on May 21, 2019.

Wilson, Ryan. "The Family-Foundation-Service-Plan: Phillip Lindsay's Vision for after NFL Involves a Police Career, Taekwondo."CBS Sports (cbssports.com). November 9, 2018.

Woelk, Neill. "Buffs' Lindsay Took Dedication, Work Ethic to Classroom as Well as Football Field." Colorado Buffaloes (cubuffs.com). May 9, 2018.

Woods, Jon. "Phillip Lindsay Officially a Colorado Buffalo." SB Nation: The Ralphie Report (ralphiereport.com). February 6, 2013.

PHOTOGRAPHY CREDITS